William Pindar

A Sermon of Divine Providence

In the Special Preservation of Government and Kingdoms, on Ps. CXXVII. 1

.

William Pindar

A Sermon of Divine Providence
In the Special Preservation of Government and Kingdoms, on Ps. CXXVII. 1

ISBN/EAN: 9783337184506

Printed in Europe, USA, Canada, Australia, Japan

Cover: Foto ©Lupo / pixelio.de

More available books at **www.hansebooks.com**

A

SERMON

OF

Divine Providence,

In the Special Preservation

OF

GOVERNMENT

AND

KINGDOMS,

On *Pfal.* CXXVII. 1.

By WILLIAM PINDAR, *late Fellow of University-Colledg in* Oxford, *and Chaplain to the Right Honourable* Ford, *Lord* Grey *of* Werke.

Publifhed on the Difcovery of the Late PLOT.

LONDON: Printed by *M. Clark,* for *H. Brome,* at the Gun in S. *Paul's* Church-yard near the Weft-end. MDCLXXIX.

A

SERMON

ON

Pſal. CXXVII. 1.

—— *Except the Lord keep the City, the Watchman*
waketh but in vain.

ING *Solomon*, to whom this
Pſalm is intitled, doth in the
beginning of it aſſume the
perſon of an *Eccleſiaſtes*, ad-
dreſſes his diſcourſe to the
people, and inſtructs them
who is to be the object of their truſt and de-
pendance; or if King *David* made it for the v. Jun. & Trem.
in loc.
uſe of his Son (whom he deſigned to leave his
Succeſſor in the Kingdom, and therefore took
care to inſtruct him early, who was to be his,
and the Kingdoms Keeper) he inculcates upon him the ſame leſſon; by ſhewing the being, and neceſſity of Gods Providence, in or-

der

der to the good regiment of all humane affairs, and to the accomplifhing of thofe defigns which men have under the Sun ; without which, thofe means will not be able to produce their ends, which yet feem very accommodate to them , and in moft mens account, might be thought fufficient to effect them. *For except the Lord build the houfe they labour in vain that build it.* Men may take a great deal of pains to very little purpofe, unlefs God profper the work of their hands ; though they dig deep, lay the foundations of the ftructure they defign, upon a rock, and fo *build their neft very high* ; yet if God fpeak the word, the rock trembles, the building fhakes, and then as the Prophet faith, *The ftone fhall fly out of the wall, and the beam out of the timber fhall anfwer it.* Nor is Gods Providence lefs neceffary to the profpering the defigns of our heads, then it is to the accomplifhment of the works of our hands: For as a City cannot be built without him, fo nor will it ftand long unlefs he eftablifh it ; nor can it be upheld in peace, or defended in war, unlefs he protect and keep it ; no provident circumfpection and watchfulnefs of the Magiftrates, no care and diligence of the Minifters that attend them , and execute their commands, can fecure it from fecret Enemies,

or

Hab. ii. 9.

Ver. 11.

or from open violences, unlefs God be pleafed to fuperintend and watch over it; *For except the Lord keep the city, the watchman waketh but in vain.* And as the Pfalmift teacheth us that neither the private nor public adminiftration of affairs can profper without Gods bleffing; fo in the three following verfes the remaining part of this *Pfalm,* he informs us that the very continuance and fucceffion of Families muft be afcribed to the fame caufe; *For loe children* (faith he) *and the fruit of the womb are an heritage and gift, that cometh of the Lord.* That they are at all made and born into the world, and that they live in it, to bear up their Fathers Name and Family, comes peculiarly from the benediction of God, *this is a gift that cometh of the Lord.* So that the main point which the Text recommends to us, is the neceffity of Gods care and providence to the prefervation of all Government, and public Societies, and without it the infufficiency of all other means to preferve them from ruine under the fimilitude of a *Watchman,* who was ufed to be placed upon fome eminent Tower of the City; fometimes in time of Peace, always in time of War, both by day and by night, to give notice of any Enemies approach againft the City, or of any fudden evil, fuch as Fire or the like, fpringing up within it. And in the handling of this Subject,

2 Sam. xviii.
24, 25.
2 Kings ix. 17.
Ef. xxi. 11.

I shall offer thefe things to your confideration.

I. *That it is God that keeps the City, or the con-*
cern that God's Providence hath in the prefervation
of Government, and all publick Societies ; and this
Point is implied in the Text.

II. *The infufficiency of all other means, or any*
thing that men can do to prejerve the public welfare,
unlefs God's Providence be pleafed to fuperintend and
keep it ; and this is fully exprefled, Except the
Lord, *&c.*

III. *The great obligation incumbent upon us to*
engage God's care to watch over the public by endea-
vouring to make our felves worthy of fuch a keeper ;
and this Point is inferred, and it is that Ufe which
we are to make of the Premiffes.

1. It is God who keeps the City, his Providence is concerned in the prefervation of
Government, and all publick Societies.

As foon as God had by his Almighty Word
created the World, and made his eternal
Power, Wifdom, and Goodnefs illuftrious, in
this moft auguft and beautiful Temple which
he erected to his honour ; although he furnifhed it with its *portion of Goods*, gave it fufficient ablities to perform all the offices of
its nature ; yet he did not *manumit* it, and as
if he forefaw that he fhould be otherwife em-
ployed, or that bufinefs would interrupt the
stream

ftream of his happinefs, did he refolve to
take no further care of it; but as he knew
that by the law of its nature it was dependant
upon him, fo did he always defign to reign
over it, to fuftain, and uphold it, and to make
his Name more glorious, and his Attributes
yet more illuftrious in his Government of it.
The continuance of all things as they were from the 2 Pet. iii. 4.
beginning of the creation, the regular motions of
the Heavens, the conftant returns of *Summer*
and Winter, feed-time and harveft, day and night, in Gen. viii. 22.
their proper feafons; the alternate mutations of
bodies, and the fafety of the univerfe, notwithftanding the mutual oppofitions of contrary
material Principles, doth manifeft, that the
world is no more governed, then it was made
by chance, but *that the Lord hath prepared his* Pfal. ciii. 19.
throne in the heavens, and that his Kingdom ruleth lix. 13.
over all, that he ruleth in Jacob, and unto the ends
of the world.

Nor doth he only as the common Father of
the world, extend his care and providence to
his whole Creation, but he more particularly
exercifes it about the concerns of his rational
off-fpring; and yet more peculiarly about
them, as they are linked together into feveral
Societies, and by the benefit of wholfome
Laws, prudently formed into various Govern-

ments : for for these it is that the Text insinu-
ates God hath a more especial regard, *For it is
he that keepeth the City*, that watcheth over the
Nation, and preserves the publick weal of the
Kingdom, and that, both from the secret machinations of intestine Adversaries, and from
the open violences of Foreign Enemies.

1. It is God who preserves the Government
from suffering any notable change, or dissolution, by the secret machinations of home-
bred Adversaries.

There never was, nor, considering the pre-
sent constitution of humane nature, probably
can be, such a Government contrived, and
managed, as will give content and satisfaction
to all its Members ; for suppose men could
agree to new-model every Government, e-
ven after the *Platonic* or *Eutopian* order ; be-
cause a very few persons, in comparison of
the rest, can but have a share in the Legisla-
tive or Executive power of it, therefore will
a great many in all likelihood be disquieted,
that some share doth not fall to their Lot, who,
it may be, will think themselves as able to govern as they are, who ingross the Dominion to
themselves.

Numb. xxvi.
11. For this very reason we know, that *Corah*
and his Company gainsaid Gods own constitution ;

tion ; and it is natural for ambitious and afpi-
ring men in fuch circumftances (of whom
there is good ftore in every Kingdom) partly
out of revenge, and partly out of hopes to rife
by a change, to oppofe themfelves to the efta-
blifhed Government ; befides, thofe advanta-
ges of honour, and reputation, and wealth,
which are the ufual rewards of them that bear
Rule, will but raife the envy and anger of many men who will think themfelves hardly dealt
with, that they have not the fame opportunity
of being confiderable in the world ; and this
will kindle in them great defires of change,
and make them watchful to apprehend any oc-
cafion wherein they may effect it.   Add to
this, that oftentimes there are fo many private
interefts driving on, contrary to that of the
publick ; and many mens tempers and difpo-
fitions are frequently fo oppofite to that which
is requifite to make them peaceable and Loyal
Subjects ; and fometimes a Magiftrate may
do things that will be harfh and ungrateful to
the Subject ; men are naturally fo ready to
fhake off any yoke that is troublefome to
them, and very defirous to enjoy an unbound-
ed liberty ; many men are fo weary of that
which they have been accuftomed to enjoy,
and fo defirous of change and Novelty, fan-
cying

cying to themselves great happiness in another turn : These things being well considered, we cannot but fay, that it is *God who keeps the City*, from being ruined, by these inward causes of dissolution; that it is an illustrious argument of the Providence of God, that Government and Society is preserved in the world, notwithstanding that so many men by interest, by inclination, by humour, are still concerned to disturb it.

King *David*, who understood very well the art of Government, praises God upon this account, and acknowledgeth this Salvation as his own wonderful work: *Praise waiteth for thee, O God, in Sion.——Thou shalt shew us wonderful things in thy righteousness, O God of our Salvation.——For thou stillest the raging of the Seas, the noise of its Waves, and the madness of the people*, even of that people, who being considered under the former circumstances seems as ungovernable as the vast Ocean, and yet are by the wise and powerful Providence of God so secretly over-ruled, as to pay due subjection to Government, or at least hindred from giving any great disturbance to it; *For though the waves of the sea be mighty, yet the Lord who dwelleth on high is mightier.*

And this God doth, *i. e.* preserve Government

Psal. lxv. 1.

Ver. 5.

Ver. 7.

Psal. xciii. 5.

ment from diſſolution by inteſtine Adverſaries, ſometimes by turning the Counſels of the
Conſpirators into fooliſhneſs, as he did that
of *Achitophel*; and by making the hidden things
of darkneſs be ſtrangely brought to light, as
in the caſe of the *Powder-Plot* : And when a
Conſpiracy is ripened into actual Rebellion,
he ſtops it; ſometimes by taking off the prin-
cipal perſon concerned in the Defection, as in
the caſe of *Abſalom,* of *Sheba the Son of Bichri,* 2 Sam. xx. 22.
and of *Wat Tyler*; ſometimes by diſpoſing the
minds of the people to return to their duty, as
by *David's* meſſage to the men of *Judah,* after 1 Sam. xix. 14.
the Rebellion of his Son; and as was done by
an Apologue handſomly applied to the Com-
mons of *Rome* by *Menenius Agrippa.*

And as God doth by his Providence preſerve Government from ruin by the ſecret Machinations or open tumults of inteſtine Enemies : ſo,

II.   It is he alſo that preſerves it from the
open Violences of forein Adverſaries.

For God is in a peculiar manner ſtyled in
Holy Writ *the Lord of Hoſts,* the ſole Arbiter
of the ſucceſs of War; it is he alone *who ſcat-* Pſal. lxviii. 30.
tereth the people who delight in it; he that maketh Pſal. xlvi. 9.
wars to ceaſe in all the world, that breaketh the bow,
and knappeth the ſpear in ſunder, and burneth the

B   *chariots*

chariots in the fire : It is he that can put a hook in the nofe, and a bridle in the lips of a proud and infolent Enemy, and can turn him back by the way by which he came. When the

Ifa.xxxvii.29. haughty King of *Affyria* boafted the extent of his Conquefts, God tells him how it came to pafs that his Arms had been fo profperous;

2.Kings xix. 25. *Haft thou not heard long ago how I have done it, and of ancient times that I have formed it ? Now have I brought it to pafs that thou fhouldeft be to lay waft fenced cities into ruinous heaps.* But when this

Ifa. x.5. *rod of Gods anger,* and the *ftaff of his indignation,* had done the work which God had appointed him , then did he *punifh the fruit of*

Ver. 12. *the ftout heart of the King of Affyria, and the glory of his high looks* , and after a wonderful manner delivered *Jerufalem* out of his hands.

And it fometimes has gracioufly pleafed Almighty God to magnifie his power in the perfervation of a people when a potent Enemy has been ready to devour them, and there has appear'd no probable humane way of efcaping his fury. For when things feem to be defperate, all help has failed them, and fcarce

Gen. xxii. 14. hope is left behind, then *Jehovah-jireh,* it is Gods time of appearing with fuccour, and *in the mount will the Lord be feen ;* then as the *Pfal-*

Pfal. x. 14. *mift* expreffes it, when *the poor committeth him-*
felf

felf unto him, doth God take the matter into his hand; for he is the helper of the friend-lefs.

When one Nation becomes a fcourge to another, takes their fortreffes, vanquifhes their powers, and treads them down as the mire in the ftreets; though the Conqueror may be only driving on the ends of his own ambition, malice, revenge and covetoufnefs, (for which God will take a time to reckon with him,) yet doth he all this while carry on the great defign Ifa. x. 6, 7. &) of Gods Providence, and is only the minifter of His vengeance, which He by him pours out upon that people againft whom he is fent; and in this execution he cannot go beyond the Commiffion which God hath given him; He puts bounds to the raging of the Sea, and to the fury of men, and they cannot exceed thofe terms which he hath fet them. So then, that a peoples Enemies do not prevail againft them, or if they do prevail, that they do not make a full end of them, and *the confumption doth not* Ver. 21. *overflow in judgment,* is folely to be afcribed to the good Providence of God, which is the great defence of a Nation: *For it is the Lord who keeps the city.*

And the greatnefs of this bleffing, that God fhould have fuch a fpecial concern for the pre-

B 2   fervation

fervation of publick Peace and Order, and
Government, and efpecially from the evil
Machinations of inteftine Enemies, will appear by confidering thefe two particulars ; and
which may pafs alfo for fuch reafons of his
Providence, as may make the Wifdom of his
doings confpicuous to us.

1. Becaufe the world would not be otherwife tolerably habitable, if Gods Providence
did not watch over it, and preferve that Authority in it which he had conferred on the
Magiftrate. We may as well imagin that a
Ship could live at Sea in a great tempeft, when
it is toffed among rocks and quickfands, and
wants a Pilot to manage her ; as that Societies
made up of men of different interefts, of di-
ftracted minds, of boifterous paffions and ex-
travagant humours, fhould yet flourifh and
be upheld in peace and fafety, if the great
Governour of the world did not oppofe himfelf to thofe overflowings of ungodlinefs, and
took care to preferve that order which himfelf
had conftituted : If he by whom Kings reign,
did not fuftein and uphold Government, and
defend that Authority by his Providence which
he has derived to Magiftrates his Deputies in
adminiftring the affairs of his natural Kingdom ; all Societies would fall in pieces, and
confufion

confufion and mifery would cover the face of
the earth. For how fhould Juftice be admi-
niftred, where the Magiftrates Authority is not
owned, where every mans will is the meafure.
of right and wrong, and where it is accounted
no duty to be obedient to Laws? How fhould
property be preferved, where all inclofures are
broken down, every mans right is invaded,
and the diftinctions between fuperiors and in-
feriors are confounded? How fhould a Kingdom ftand, when the Pillars thereof are un-
dermined, Religion is exploded, mutual Truft
and Fidelity is derided, the offices of Charity
are neglected, and men let themfelves loofe to
all licentioufnefs? But thus it would be, if
God fhould relax the reins of Government,
withdraw for a while his providential Care
and Goodnefs, which mainteins and defends
it, and leave things to be ordered by the turbu-
lent and contrary humours of degenerate men.
Alas, *who could live, if God fhould do this?* If Numb. xxiv.
he fhould not reign as King, the flouds would 23.
lift up their waves, and rage horribly, and no
humane power could be able to fay unto them,
Peace, be ftill. And therefore the bleffing muft Pfal. xciii. 4, 5.
needs be great, by which Order and Happinefs
are preferved amongft us, and the world becomes an habitation fit for us.

2. By this means alſo all our own ſtudy, and care, and induſtry that is laid out upon the preſervation of the publick is not in vain, but effect thoſe ends to which ſuch means are deſigned; for the work muſt ſucceed which God hath proſpered, when he keeps the city, the watchman waketh to very good purpoſe. And therefore upon the conſideration of this great bleſſing, that Gods Providence watcheth over a Nation for good, we are kept off from all deſpondency touching the iſſue of our own labours about the ſame end; we are taught to rely upon him who is All-ſufficient, and encouraged to uſe all rational means to preſerve our ſelves, becauſe God keeping us, they cannot be in vain. So that being ſecured of Gods Providence, we have all imaginable aſſurance given us, that if we be intent upon the doing of our duties for the preſervation of the publick, the Body Politick will be preſerved in a good Athletick frame and temper: For as God doth not uſe to work miracles to preſerve the careleſs and the diſſolute, who neglect the ordinary means of their ſafety; ſo nor doth his Providence ordinarily forſake them, who uſe all the care that becomes them for the ſecuring of themſelves, and then reſign themſelves to the Divine will and pleaſure.

I

I ſhould now paſs on to the ſecond Particular, but that it is fit that I ſhould ſay ſomething in anſwer to an Objection, which will ſpring up in every ones mind upon his hearing of the Premiſſes. For if God thus keep the City, that is, has ſuch a care for Government, as has been declared, then how comes it to paſs that Government is ſometimes overturned by the arms of a proſperous rabble, that a flouriſhing Nation is ſomtimes brought to ruin by the evil devices of Inteſtine, and ſometimes by the invaſion of Foreign Enemies ? How comes God to permit wickedneſs to poſſeſs the place _Eccl. iii. 16._ of judgment, and iniquity the place of righteouſneſs ? all civil and ſacred rights to be invaded, and nothing but confuſion and deſolation to be ſpread over a Nation.

For anſwer to which doubts it muſt be conſidered, That a Nation may by their ſins forfeit all the right it had to Gods providential care and Protection over it ; ſo that he may in juſtice leave it to be puniſht by the malice and rage of its enemies, and uſe them as his rod, to ſcourge the wickedneſs of a perverſe and rebellious people. That God has frequently _Gen. xv. 16._ dealt thus with ſeveral publick Communities, _Lev. xviii. 24,_ when their ſins have been ripe for vengeance, _25. Deut. xxxii._ the Hiſtories of his dealings with ſeveral Nati- _19. 2 Kings xvii. 6, 7, 18._

ons

2 Chro.xxxvi.
14, 17.
St. Luke xix.
41, 42, 43, 44.
1 Thef. ii. 15,
16.
ons fet down in the Holy Scriptures, make clearly evident.   And that there is very good reafon that he ftill fhould do fo in the like ca- fes, that is, punifh a Nation feverely, when its fins reach heaven, and fomtimes blot it out from under it, when it is paft all remedy, will appear evident alfo to the fober confiderer of thefe following things : For,

1. Thefe dealings of God vindicate the ho- nour of his Attributes before all men, and give clear demonftration of his impartial Ju- ftice and Providence to the world.   It may be the people over whom God extended his care, and made them dwell at eafe, *facrificed to their own net, and burnt incenfe to their drag*, afcri- bed their profperity to their own policies, and thought that their fuccefs was the fole product of their own wifdom and induftry ; or it may be, they begun to think God fuch a one as themfelves, that their profperity was an ap- probation of their wickednefs, that the refpite of judgment was the remiffion of their guilt, and becaufe the Divine fentence was not exe- cuted, therefore they were acquitted, and *their* Eccl. viii. 11. *hearts* thereupon *fully fet in them to do evil.* Thus thofe Scoffers whom St. *Peter* defcribed (2 *Ep.* 3.) thought the evil day was far from them, indeed fo far, as that it would never over-

overtake them, ſince all things continued as they always were, they ask, Where is Gods promiſe of his coming to judgment? It may be the impunity of ſuch a people does at length become a ſcandal to their neighbours, and they begin to cry out, *Why does the way of the wicked* Jer. xii. 1. *proſper? Wherefore are they happy that deal very treacherouſly?* And in theſe or the like caſes, it is but neceſſary that God ſhould convince them and the world, by a Demonſtration *à poſteriori,* how much they were miſtaken in their notions of Him and his Providence; ſince now he means to aſſert his own honour by making ſuch a people as notorious for their puniſhments, as they had been infamous for their crimes. For thus did God reſolve to vindicate himſelf and the former methods of his Providence in the overthrow of the *Egyptians, I will get me honour* (ſaith he) *upon Pharaoh and* Exod. xiv. 17, *upon all his hoſt, and the Egyptiaans ſhall know that* 18. *I am the Lord,* &c.

2. Kingdoms as ſuch, are only capable of being thus puniſhed by God in this life, in being bereaved of all thoſe bleſſings which make them a happy and a flouriſhing Nation. This is the time of recompence to them; the rewards or puniſhments of the other life being there only to be meaſured out to every ſingle

perſon, according to the things that he has done in the body, whether it be good or bad.

3. God makes public Judgments become common Antidotes againſt the poiſon of wickedneſs, by disburthening the world of that heavy load of incorrigible ſinners that oppreſſeth it; and making poſterity afraid of imitating their vices, out of hopes of impunity, when they have ſeen that ſin in the end has become ſo great a reproach to a people, *that it has only brought forth the poiſon of dragons, and the cruel venom of aſps.* The *Iſraelites* whom God had owned in *Egypt* for his own peculiar people, and delivered them thence, from the houſe of bondage, with a mighty hand, and ſo as to make his name renowned among all the Nations, and was carrying them through the Wilderneſs towards the land of Promiſe; yet their frequent rebellions againſt God in the Wilderneſs, made him *ſwear in his wrath, that they ſhould not enter into his reſt;* and accordingly none of them did enter into *Canaan,* ſave *Caleb* and *Joſhua* : but God made them ſojourn in the wilderneſs forty years, that thoſe incorrigible ſinners might be cut off, and a better generation of men might be grown up, to poſſeſs the land which God had provided for them.

Deut. xxxii. 33.

Heb. xi. 3.

Numb. xiv. 30.

Pub-

Public Afflictions are the laſt Remedies
which God uſeth for the curing of public Ma-
ladies; but when the methods of his Patience
fail, and he is weary with bearing, then the
nature of the diſtemper, and the ends of his
Government require, that he ſhould lay the
ax to the root, and the fan to the floor, and
that he ſhould burn up the chaff with un-
quenchable Fire.   This account of Gods deal-
ing with *Judah* doth the ſacred Hiſtory give
us; *And the Lord God of their fathers ſent unto* 2 Chro.xxxvi,
them by his meſſengers, riſing up betimes and ſending, 15, 16, 17.
becauſe he had compaſſion on his people and on his
dwelling-place : but they mocked the meſſengers of
God, and deſpiſed his words, and miſuſed his pro-
phets, until the wrath of the Lord aroſe againſt his
people, till there was no remedy; therefore he brought
upon them the King of the Chaldees, &c.
   It is true, in all National Judgments, good
men oftentimes bear their ſhare, as well as the
wicked ; for they are all equally members of
the ſame *Body Politic,* and therefore the ſame di-
ſtempers of State will affect them both.   But
this ſtill makes a calamity become far the more
grievous to the Public, in that thoſe men that
are the ſalt of Society and keep it from putre-
faction, thoſe that by the fervency of their
Prayers and the holineſs of their Lives kept

off Gods judgments for a long time; and when the divine difpleafure begins to arife, do as *Mofes* ftand in the gap, and mediate for the people, that the whole Nation perifh not; that thefe men are fwept away in a common

Pfal. lxxv. 4. calamity, that bear up *the pillars of the earth*, is very inaufpicious to the Public, and augments their miferies. God would have faved *Sodom* for ten righteous, and it is for the fake of good men (the Rabbins fay) that the world is pre-ferved; to fee them therefore perifh in the

Ifa. ix. 12, 17.
21. common fate is a fad inftance, that *Gods anger is not turned away, but that his hand will be ftretched out ftill.*

4. National fins by a natural efficacy pro-duce publick miferies; fit and difpofe a State

Lev. xiv. 44,
45. for its diffolution. They are like the *fretting le-profie in an houfe*, which diffufes its venom through every part of the building, and the plague is not to be cured, but by rafing it to the foundation. Thus fell the Jewifh State by the *Romans*; thus did the *Greek* Empire lofe its glory and fplendor, and *Mahomet* prevailed; and thus the *Britains* (faith *Gildas Sapiens*) were loft, when the *Saxons* invaded them. And this every Nation tends to naturally, ac-cording to the prevalency that Idlenefs and Luxury, Pride and Intemperance and Factiouf-nefs have over them.   While

" While States and Commonwealths have Bacon, Adv. of Learn. l. 4. c. 2. p. 131.
" been in their growth and rifing, Arts Milita-
" ry have flourifhed; when they have been fet-
" tled and ftood at a height, Arts Liberal ; and
" drawing to their declenfion and ruin, Arts
" Voluptuary.

And thus briefly I have endeavoured to give fome account, why, notwithftanding Gods great care and concern for the prefervation of Government, and public Society, yet a flourifhing Nation may be fometimes ruined by Rebels from within, or by the invafion of a potent Enemy from without.

I come now to confider the fecond particular, and which is exprefled in the Text, *viz.* The Infufficiency of all other means or any thing that men can do to preferve the public welfare, unlefs Gods Providence be pleafed to fuperintend and keep it : For *except the Lord keep the city,* &c.

And this Point, namely, *That all that men can do will not be able to fecure the publick welfare, unlefs God be on their fide, and keep it;* ftands upon thefe four following Reafons.

Firft, Becaufe the over-ruling hand of Gods Providence orders all the affairs of the world as it beft pleafes him ; and this I think is clear in that I have faid upon the firft parti

C 3　　　　cular;

cular ; and if it be fo, then the confequence
of it muft be alfo evident, *viz*. That the public welfare cannot be preferved without his
bleffing, by whofe guidance all things are ordered, without whofe concourfe nothing can
be effected, upon whofe difpofal all fuccefs
dependeth. For how fhould we profper, if
God be not on our fide ? Are we ftronger than
he ? Can we wreft the Government out of his
Ifa. ix. hand, by our policies out-wit the *mighty Coun-*
fellor, or weary him by refiftance, to whom
Pfal. lxii. 11. *power alone belongeth* ? Or if God be not for us,
can we think that he will not be againft us ?
Do we fuppofe that God will ftand *neuter*, an
unconcern'd fpectator of all human affairs that
are reprefented upon the theatre of this world ;
not caring who wins the prize, nor who becomes a prey to a powerful and cruel enemy ?
Is there no intereft but our own going on in the
world ? Has not God the great ends of his Wifdom, Juftice and Goodnefs to promote, the
glory of his Name and Attributes to fecure, by
his providential difpenfations ? Yes of this we
may be well affured, that God is abfolute and
fupreme in his authority, wife and righteous
in all his ways, and that he who made all
things by the word of his power, will rule and
govern them fo as to illuftrate his Glory, and
                                          accom-

accompliſh his ends by the power of his Providence.

Secondly, All that men can do will not be
able to preſerve the public welfare, unleſs
God be pleaſed to keep it; becauſe our under-
ſtandings are too ſhallow, our powers too little, our lives too ſhort and uncertain, to compaſs any conſiderable deſigns, or to do thoſe
things that will ſecure a Nation, without the
bleſſing of Gods Providence. For,

(1.) The wiſeſt Politicians cannot certainly foreſee what things may riſe in their way to
ſtop the attainment of their ends, ſo cannot
tell what means to furniſh themſelves with,
that may be able to remove thoſe obſtacles.
Men cannot bring about their deſigns, but by
means that are proper and adequate to them;
what means will be ſo they cannot certainly
tell, unleſs they could alſo know what impe-
diments they muſt remove, before they can
compaſs their ends : this cannot be known,
unleſs they could foreſee all thoſe poſſible acci-
dents, which may ſuddenly ſpring up contrary to their deſigns; but ſuch foreſight is beyond
the ſphere of a human intellect : The wiſeſt
man can but gueſs probably in ſome things, he
may be to ſeek in many, and it is poſſible that
he may be miſtaken in all. A deſign may go
on.

on very glibly for fome time, when on a fudden fome undifcernible accident arifes, which mars the project, though very finely fpun, ftops the Politician in the midft of his career, and then *the wife are taken in their own craftinefs.* *Machiavel* obferves it of *Cæfar Borgia* (the bafe Son of Pope *Alexander* VI. whom for his Policy he propofes as a fit pattern for Princes,) that he had confidered and forefeen all the confequences that his Fathers fudden death might produce; and accordingly was fo well prepared for fuch an accident, that his Enemies, of whom he had good ftore, fhould not be able to do him any great damage upon it, or to influence the Conclave contrary to his interefts. But he, as cunning as he was, did not forefee nor provide againft that fudden accident which did fall out, and which was his ruin; for he did not confider that himfelf might be fick, as he was, when his Father died fuddenly of that very Poifon which they had both prepared for them that they hated, and which was given to themfelves by miftake; upon which account he could not in that exigent look after his affairs, but was forced to fhift for his life, which he after loft unlamented. *Thus* (as *Eliphaz* faith) *did God difappoint the devices of the crafty, fo that their hands could not perform their enterprife.*

Job v. v. 12.

From

From what fmall and contemptible begin-
nings have the greateft matters that could concern the public rifen ! Upon what flender and
fecret hinges have the fates of whole Nations turned ! Who would have thought that
Mafaniello a poor fimple Fifherman, fhould
have in a few days time gained an abfolute un-
limited power over the City of *Naples*, and
caufed fuch revolutions in it, as fcarce any Hi-
ftory can parallel ? And how was it poffible
for the wifeft Statefman to have forefeen, and
to have been furnifhed with means to have
prevented fuch an accident ?

God indeed can certainly forefee the moft
minute and remote contingencies that can poffibly arife about any affair ; he can bring about
his ends without means, or by very unlikely
ones ; he fometimes *chufes the foolifh things of* 1 Cor. i 27,28.
the world to confound the wife, the weak things of
the world to confound the things which are mighty ;
and the bafe things of the world and things which are
defpifed, and things which are not, to bring to nought
things that are. Thus did he baffle the counfel
of *Achitophel*, which was accounted *as wife as* 2 Sam. xvi. 23.
if a man fhould have enquired of the oracle of God, ch. xvii.
with the worfe counfel of *Hufhai*. He made
Haman minifter to the honour and advance-
ment of him whom he moft hated, *Mordecai* ; Efth. vi, vii.

D   and

and afterwards ruin'd him with his own project, and he was taken in the crafty wilyness that he had imagined. He at the fame time delivered the Jews in captivity. when they were upon the brink of ruin, even after they had been devoted to it by *Ahafuerus* himself. So great, fo efficacious is the Divine Wifdom.

But now men are pofed with every difficulty that arifes, and even when they have gone a great way toward their defign, and a little crofs unforefeen accident emerges, it puts them to their wits end, and dafhes all their hopes of fuccefs in a moment : For *malum ex quolibet defectu* is here alfo found true; if one link be but broken in this chain of confequences, the defired Conclufion will never be inferred.

(2.) Our powers are very little, our hands are too weak to effect all thofe things which even our wifdom tells us are neceffary to be done in order to the fecurity of the Public Weal; and we muft be forced to venture much of our affair in another bottom, and commit our bufinefs to Inftruments, which can act as freely as our felves, and not only fo far as they are influenced by us. We cannot fay to them, as God does to the waters of the Sea, *Hitherto fhall ye come, and no further* : We cannot bound their

their operations, for they are free and not natural Agents; and being fo, they may feveral ways fpoil the faireft defign we can poffibly engage in. But admit our Inftruments fhould prove wife and faithful, yet ftill our powers would be too little, unlefs we could either fo keep under our enemies, that they fhould not be able to obftruct our affairs; or fo to influence them, as to make them promote them. For although neither the power nor the cunning of our enemies fhould be equal to ours, yet if their malice be great, that may make them very vigilant to gain an opportunity, wherein they may do moft prejudice to our affairs.

God indeed can make his enemies ferviceable to his ends, he can make them do His bufinefs, when they think moft certainly that they are driving on their own. When through envy the Brethren of *Jofeph* fold him into *Egypt*; this they thought was an effectual courfe to prove the vanity of his dreams, and to prevent their falling down before him and worfhipping him; when loe by that very action God was making way for his exaltation to the Government of *Egypt*, and fo for the certain accomplifhment of his dreams: and when through falfe accufation he was caft into prison, this was but one farther step towards his Advancement. When *Judas* betrayed, *Pilate* condemned, and the *Jews* crucified the Lord of Life, every one of them was driving on their several interests ; *Judas*, that he might get money ; *Pilate*, left he should not shew himself a friend to *Cæsar*, and that he might gain the favour of the *Jews* ; the *Jews*, that they might revenge themselves upon him who had prophesied evil against them, and prevent the *Romans* from coming and taking away their Nation, upon the score of the common peoples running after *Jesus* as a *King*.

And yet God did not only blast these counsels of the wicked, and made their execrable villany so far from promoting their several ends, that it was the only thing that defeated them ; (for we know what *Judas* got by the thirty pieces the price of his Treason ; *Pilate* not long after lost *Cæsars* favour, and killed himself in his banishment ; and the *Romans* within forty years after did come and took away the *Jewish* Nation, and they, once Gods peculiar people, continue yet vagabonds upon the face of the earth:) God did not only I say defeat their several ends, by those very actions which they expected would have secured them ; but, which is the thing I aim at, he did

ac-

accomplifh his own great and glorious end by
the treafons, and confpiracies, and malice of
his bitter enemies ; an end worthy of God, to
draw the greateft good out of the greateft evil,
and by which he manifefted the glory of his
Attributes as clearly, as he did by the Creation of the world : For by the death of his Son
did he deftroy the works of the Devil, bruife
the head of that old Serpent, his firft and greateft enemy ; and fo accomplifhed the Redemp-
tion of mankind.

But now to make the force and powers of
ones enemies the proper means of accomplifhing his defigns, is the proregative of him alone
who is omnipotent ; but unto man fuch power
is not granted, as to over-rule the actions of
his enemies, and to make them in any fenfe be
fubfervient to his ends ; and then, how fhould
he, without Gods bleffing, be able to fecure
to a people their happinefs ? But further,

(3.) We are too weak and infufficient to
compafs any confiderable defigns, or to give
any lafting fecurity to the Public, becaufe of
the frailty and fhortnefs of our lives ; we cannot fecure to our felves one moments continuance in our prefent ftation, then how fhould
we be able to fecure greater matters ? We are
daily obnoxious to many cafualties which may

cut us off in the midſt of our days and buſineſs ;
which may ſurprize us unawares when we are
moſt healthful and vigorous, when we are
within the proſpect of harbour, and about to
enjoy the fruit of our labours : Inſomuch as
upon this account we cannot promiſe our-
Prov. xxvii. 1. ſelves the life of one day, becauſe *we know not
what a day may bring forth.* We are made up
and compounded of contrary principles, that
are often jarring and claſhing among one another, and threaten to us, that our abode cannot be long in theſe frail Tabernacles, though
we ſhould happily eſcape all ſad and ſudden
caſualties; nay, though upon the account of our
happy and healthful conſtitutions we might
hope to reach the ordinary age of man ; yet do
our lives wholly depend upon the good pleaſure of God, and he may require them when
he will, inſomuch as when we attempt the per-
formance of any affair, we can only ſay, as
Chap. iv. 15. St. *James* teacheth us, *If the Lord will, we ſhall
live, and do this or that ;* but this we cannot promiſe, this we muſt not build upon, without
a pious ſubmiſſion and an humble reference of
our ſelves and our affairs to the wiſe diſpoſal,
to the ſovereign will of our great Governour,
for we are not our own ; and therefore upon this
ſcore of our dependent conditions, we cannot
accom-

accomplifh any thing without his Blefling whofe we are, and by whom we fubfift. And yet after all,

(4.) Though we were much wifer and much more powerful than we are, and could affure our felves of a longer and more fteady continuance of our lives than we can ; yet all this would not do the bufinefs,the employment would be ftill too arduous to be undertaken,the work too great to be performed by Mortals ; the greateft Monarch would be crufhed under the ruins of his own Government, unlefs God upheld both him and it. *By me* (faith he) *Kings reign* ; it is by Gods fpecial appointment and defignation that Kings are his *Vice-gerents* in the world ; it is by his peculiar care and prote-ction that their authority is preferved, and that their perfons are at any time fenced and fecured, from the malicious defigns or the out-ragious violences of wicked and unreafonable men. The nature of Government is fuch, that it requires a Divine Wifdom, and an un-controulable Power to fuftein it, and to main-tein its interefts.

For he that can preferve it muft be able to penetrate into the fecret counfels of fuch as confederate againft it ; he muft not wait to know caufes by their effects, for then he may
be.

be to seek for such remedies, as are proper for
the curing of public distempers, when the
opportunity of applying them is at hand ; but
he must see the Tempest afar off, whilst it
is wrapt up in its seed and principle, and
may be covered *with a mans hand.* He must
hold the reins of mens Passions in his hands,
be able to slack their fury, and check their
impetuousness; know how to mix and com-
pound their Hopes and their Fears, their Love
and their Hatred, their Anger and their Jealou-
sies, so as to make them refract and contemper
one another : so he must extract the most sove-
reign preservative of Government out of those
things which would be its greatest bane; and
that which in its own nature is apt to disturb,
must be so managed as that it may promote
and advance publick Peace and Security.

   He that is able to discharge this Province,
Psal. cxxi. 4. *must neither slumber nor sleep,* lest the mischief
that walketh in darkness, come in an hour
when it is not expected.   He must have an
universal influence over all those second causes
whence arise great Dearths, contagious Sick-
nesses, violent Tempests, fearful Inundations;
all things wherewith the life of man is nou-
rished, preserved and defended, must be under
his disposal ; the Heavens above, and the
                                          Earth

Earth beneath, nay, the Winds and Seas, which feem leaft capable of a Law, muft obey him.

Finally, he that can manage this employment, muft, after a Nation has been broken to pieces by factions and civil difcord, after it has been caft down to the loweft degree of mifery, *fervants have ruled over it* with Lam. v. v. 8. a rod of iron, and *there was none that did deliver it out of their hands* ; he muft be able then to refcue it from utter ruine, to reunite the fhattered pieces of it into one again, to give it a Refurrection, and *make the dry bones live,* to make Ezek. xxxvii. David *his fervant King over it,* and reftore it 5. v. 24. to its priftine Glory and Liberty.

Sedition is commonly the work of mean Varlets ; a *Mafaniello* and a *Wat Tyler* can give fufficient difturbance to a lawful Government: *Rome* was moft endangered by the *Bellum Servile,* the mutiny of its Slaves ; for *behold how great a matter a little fire kindleth* : But to prevent public mifchiefs or redrefs them, to reftore lawful Powers, to eftablifh and defend our Princes as at the firft, and our Governours as at the beginning, This is indeed a great and a noble undertaking.

Thefe things the Patron, the Preferver, the Saviour of a Nation muft do, and thefe he

E   only

only can do, who has infallible Wifdom, ir-
refiftable Power, fupreme Sovereignty over
the whole world; who is intimately prefent
to every part of it, fills the whole heavens,
fitteth upon the circle of the earth, and *doth whatfo-*
ever it pleafeth him, in heaven and in earth, in the
feas and in all deep places. So that *our help cometh*
ftill from the Lord who made heaven and earth, for
it is *the Lord who is our keeper*; and *except the*
Lord keep the city, the watchman waketh but in vain.
And therefore,

Thirdly, We fee the great obligation that is
incumbent upon us to engage Gods care to
watch over the Publick, by endeavouring to
make our felves worthy of fuch a *Keeper*; and
the confideration of this is the *Ufe* we are to
make of the premiffes.

For by fome things that were difcourfed upon the firft particular, we might fee that a Nation might be in fuch circumftances, that God
would not only refufe to watch over it for
good, but he would *fet his face againft it* to deftroy it, and to make it become an *aftonifh-*
ment and a proverb among all Nations. For
God flees from the Tents of the wicked, he
knoweth the ungodly afar off, he will have no
intercourfe of Friendfhip with them, fhew no
acts of kindnefs to them, but leave them to
perifh by their own tranfgreffions.   To

Marginal notes:
Ifa. lx.
Pfal. cxxxv. 6.
Pfal. cxxi.
Lev. xxvi.
Deut. xxviii.

To prevent this great evil, and ſtill to ſecure Gods protection over us, let us put in practice that advice which the Prophet *Iſaiah* gave to his own Nation, *Waſh you, make you clean; put away the evil of your doings from before mine eyes; ceaſe to do evil, learn to do well,* &c. And then, *If ye be thus obedient, ye ſhall eat the good of the land; but if ye refuſe and rebel, ye ſhall be devoured, for the mouth of the Lord hath ſpoken it,* v. 20. Iſa. i. 15, 17. Ver. 19.

Now as there are ſome great perſonal ſins which do more than others, waſt the Conſcience, deſtroy the clearneſs, the tenderneſs, the peace of the Mind ; and which baniſh the Holy Spirit from us, and caſt us ſpeedily out of Gods preſence : So may there be alſo ſome great National ſins which may quite break the league of amity which has been between God and a people; which may incenſe him beyond all patience, oblige him to become their enemy, to give them a bill of divorce, and utterly to forſake them ; and ſuch are avowed Atheiſm, open general Profaneneſs, great abuſe of Gods Mercies, Contempt of his Word, murmuring at his Providences, mainteining Factions againſt his Government, Unthankfulneſs for Gods Bleſſings, perverting of Juſtice, oppreſſing of the Poor, and the like ; and inſtances might be given how much woe theſe have wrought to a people, where they have become National, either by the general practice, or by the practice of those in high and eminent place; or by the impunity of the guilty, when evil is not put away from a land by executing of judgment upon the Transgressors.

And therefore as we heartily desire that publick Peace and Happiness should flourish among us, it will concern every man, according to the station which God has placed him in, to avoid, discountenance, suppress and punish those wasting sins especially, which are so directly levelled against the honour of God, and the fear of His Name, shall I say? Nay, against the Majesty of the Prince, and the safety of the people; which break up the foundations of the earth, and let in a whole deluge of calamities into the world.

When God warns the Congregation of *Israel* to avoid all pollutions, he gives this reason for his injunction, *For the Lord thy God walketh in the midst of thy camp to deliver thee, therefore shall thy camp be holy, that he see no unclean thing in thee, and turn away from thee.* And there are some pollutions which will defile a whole Land, not only make God forsake it, but make it also spue out the inhabitants thereof; when a people grow impudent and incorrigible in their sins,

Margin notes:
Deut. xvii. 12.
ch. xix. 13.

Deut. xxiii. 14.

fins, *then the shew of their countenance doth wit-* Lev. xviii 25.
nefs againft them, they declare their fin as Sodom,
and hide it not ; then woe unto their fouls, for they
have rewarded evil unto themfelves, faith the Prophet.　Therefore, if we would fecure Gods Ifa.iii.9.
prefence among us, and his care over us, we
muft put away our abominations from before
his eyes, and *ceafe to do evil ;* we muft *not touch* 2 Cor. vi. 17,
the unclean thing, and then *I will be a Father unto* 18.
you, faith the Lord Almighty.

　　And becaufe God hath diftinguifhed us as it
were, from the reft of the world, by the greatnefs and multitude of his choiceft mercies ;
has fet up his kingdom among us, the Scepter
of righteoufnefs, by beftowing upon us his Holy Word and Ordinances, the means and ad-
vantages of Grace and Salvation, and the to-
kens of his fpecial prefence, having fo made
us, as St. *Peter* fpeaks, *A Royal Priefthood,* *a* 1 Ep. ii. 5.
holy nation, a peculiar people : Therefore, there
is a farther duty incumbent upon us, as we
would have the continuance of God and his
Bleffings amongft us ; and that is, That we
fhould *walk worthy of the vocation wherewith we are* Eph.iv. 1, 3.
called, endeavouring to keep the unity of the fpirit
in the bond of peace. Our *converfation muft be as it* Phil. i. 27.
becometh the Gofpel of Chrift ; we muft walk worthy Col. i. 1c.
of the Lord, unto all pleafing, being fruitful in eve-
E 3　　　　　　　　*ry*

ry good work ; For God expects, and juſtly, that his vineyard ſhould bring forth fruits anſwerable to all the care and charge wherewith it has Iſa. v. v, 2, 6. been fenced and cultivated ; or elſe he *will lay it waſt, and command the clouds, that they rain no rain upon it.* In this caſe our Lord told the Jews what uſage they were to expect from God, and what, by analogy of reaſon , ſhould be any other peoples portion, that ſhould do as they Matt. xxi. 43. did. *Therefore I ſay unto you, the Kingdom of God ſhall be taken from you, and given to a nation bringing forth the fruits thereof.* Which heavy judgment may God avert from us! and may he ſtill delight to dwell among us , to watch over us, and to bleſs us, for Jeſus Chriſt his ſake, *To whom,* &c.

Dom. 5. poſt Trin. Coll.

Grant, *O Lord, we beſeech thee , that the courſe of this world may be ſo peaceably ordered by thy governance, that thy Church may joyfully ſerve thee in all godly quietneſs, through Jeſus Chriſt our Lord.* Amen.

FINIS.

9 783337 184506